Girls Play RUGBY

Girls JOIN THE TEAM

Emma Jones

PowerKiDS press.

New York

Published in 2017 by The Rosen Publishing Group, Inc.
29 East 21st Street, New York, NY 10010

First Edition

Editor: Katie Kawa
Book Design: Tanya Dellaccio

Photo Credits: Cover, pp. 5, 11 (bottom) , 21 (top) Mai Techaphan/ Shutterstock.com; p. 7 (top) Dean Mouhtaropoulos/Getty Images; p. 7 (bottom) https:// commons.wikimedia.org/wiki/File:Women-rugby-team-australia-1930s.jpg; p. 8 dean bertoncelj/Shutterstock.com; pp. 9, 17 (bottom) Harry Engels/Getty Images; pp. 11 (top), 22 Mark Herreid/Shutterstock.com; p. 13 Harry How/Getty Images; p. 17 (top) Phil Walter/Getty Images; p. 19 David Rogers/Getty Images; p. 21 (bottom) ED JONES/AFP/Getty Images.

Cataloging-in-Publication Data

Names: Jones, Emma.
Title: Girls play rugby / Emma Jones.
Description: New York : PowerKids Press, 2017. | Series: Girls join the team | Includes index.
Identifiers: ISBN 9781499421057 (pbk.) | ISBN 9781499421071 (library bound) | ISBN 9781499421064 (6 pack)
Subjects: LCSH: Rugby football–Juvenile literature. | Rugby football for girls.
Classification: LCC GV945.25 J66 2017 | DDC 796.333–d23

Manufactured in the United States of America

CPSIA Compliance Information: Batch #BS16PK For Further Information contact Rosen Publishing, New York, New York at 1-800-237-9932

CONTENTS

A TOUGH SPORT

Rugby is a tough sport that features hard hits and big battles for the ball. For many years, most people only saw rugby as a sport for boys and men because of all the **contact** involved. However, girls and women are tough, too! Today, rugby is a popular sport for both boys and girls around the world.

Playing rugby gives girls the tools to grow into strong, smart women. There are different kinds of rugby played at many different levels. If you're interested in playing this exciting sport, it's easy to start, and it could take you all the way to the Summer Olympics!

Overtime!

Rugby has its roots in the sport of football, which is known as soccer in the United States. Different kinds of football games have been around for centuries.

Rugby is one of the few full-contact sports played by women in large numbers around the world.

PART FACT, PART LEGEND

The story of how the modern game of rugby came to be is part fact and part **legend**. It's known that a young man named William Webb Ellis attended Rugby School in England. It's also commonly told that he helped create the sport of rugby by picking up the ball and running with it during a football game in 1823. However, no one knows for sure if that's what really happened. All that's certain is rugby grew in popularity throughout the 1800s.

Rugby has been played in the United States since the early days of the sport. However, interest in rugby began to grow steadily during the 1970s. This included interest in both men's rugby and women's rugby.

Overtime!

The USA Women's Eagles—the U.S. national women's rugby team—was founded in 1987.

Because of the tough nature of rugby, many people believed it wasn't a sport women should play. While some women's teams started playing the sport earlier in its history, it wasn't until the 1980s that women's rugby really began to grow.

women's rugby team in the 1930s

THE LAWS OF RUGBY

Rugby is a sport that exercises your brain as well as your body. It has many rules, which are called laws, to remember as you play. The object of the game is to score points by moving the ball over the goal line. A rugby ball can be moved in three ways. Players can kick it, run with it, or pass it. However, they can only pass it backward.

Lines called touch lines run the length of a rugby field, or pitch. If the ball goes over one of those lines, the other team can throw the ball back into play between two lines of players. This is called a line-out.

Overtime!

A rugby ball is shaped like an oval. It looks like an American football, but its ends aren't as pointy. This shape makes it hard to figure out where it's going to **bounce** when it hits the ground!

Because the sidelines in rugby are called touch lines, when the ball goes over one of them and out of play, it's said to be "in touch." This stops the game, and a line-out, shown here, allows the game to start again. Line-outs only happen in certain kinds of rugby.

WHAT'S A SCRUM?

One of the most recognizable parts of a rugby match, or game, is the scrum. A scrum can happen after one team loses possession of the ball and it goes forward. This is called a knock-on. After a knock-on or another stoppage of play, play can start again with a scrum. During a scrum, a group of players from both teams form a tight group. The ball is thrown into the group, and the players try to get possession of it by pushing each other and using their feet.

Rugby players are generally divided into two groups. The forwards, or pack, form a scrum. The backs stand behind the scrum.

Overtime!

One way rugby players can lose the ball is by being tackled. When a player is tackled, she has to let go of the ball.

When many people think of rugby, they think of a scrum. However, that's just one small part of a rugby match.

SHE SCORES!

Not all scoring plays in rugby lead to the same number of points. The play that earns the most points is called a try. This play happens when a player touches the ball down on or over the other team's goal line. In some kinds of rugby, it's worth four points, and in others, it's worth five.

Points can also be scored in rugby by kicking the ball. A team can score an extra two points after a try on a conversion. This happens when the ball is kicked through the goalposts. A penalty kick is taken the same way if the other team breaks certain rules. The resulting penalty goal is worth two or three points, depending on the kind of rugby being played.

Overtime!

A drop goal is another way to score in rugby. It happens when a player drops the ball during a game and kicks it through the goalposts as it bounces off the ground.

Scoring plays in rugby are **similar** to scoring plays in American football. A try is like a touchdown, and the kicking plays are like field goals and extra-point kicks.

13

LEAGUE, UNION, AND SEVENS

There are three main kinds of rugby. Rugby league is a kind of rugby played with 13 players on each team. In rugby league, a try is worth four points, a penalty goal is worth two points, and a drop goal is worth one point.

Rugby union is played with 15 players on each team. Rugby sevens features teams of seven players. In both of these kinds of rugby, a try is worth five points, and both penalty goals and drop goals are worth three points. Rugby union and rugby sevens are the most popular kinds of rugby played by women around the world.

Overtime!

Women's rugby league is played mainly in Great Britain, Australia, and New Zealand.

RUGBY GLOSSARY

conversion

An extra kick made after the ball goes over the other team's goal line that is always worth two points if successful.

knock-on

A loss of possession when the ball goes forward.

line-out

A way to restart play after the ball goes out of bounds by throwing it back onto the field between two lines of players.

maul

A play that happens when a player carrying the ball is stopped but not brought to the ground, so the fight for the ball happens with all players standing and moving.

ruck

A play that happens when players fight for possession of the ball with their feet while standing and holding on to each other. Unlike a scrum, a ruck happens during play and not to restart play.

rugby league

Rugby played with 13 players on each team.

rugby sevens

Rugby played with seven players on each team.

rugby union

Rugby played with 15 players on each team.

try

A scoring play that happens when a player from one team touches the ball down on or over the other team's goal line.

Rugby is a game that uses some crazy words! These are some of the most common words used when talking about rugby and what they mean.

RUGBY AROUND THE WORLD

Rugby sevens became an Olympic sport in 2016 when it was played during the Summer Olympics in Rio de Janeiro, Brazil. The best men's and women's rugby sevens players from around the world **competed** in this Olympic event.

There are international **competitions** for rugby league and rugby union, too. The highest level of these international competitions is called a World Cup. The USA Women's Eagles program has both a rugby sevens team and a rugby union team. The Women's Eagles rugby union team won the first official Women's Rugby World Cup in 1991. New Zealand holds the record with four World Cup wins.

Overtime!

New Zealand's national women's rugby union team, which is called the Black Ferns, won its four World Cups in a row—in 1998, 2002, 2006, and 2010.

Women's rugby wasn't an Olympic sport before the 2016 Summer Olympics.

New Zealand Black Ferns

USA Women's Eagles

A WORLD CUP CAPTAIN

One of the most famous players on New Zealand's Black Ferns national team was Farah Palmer. Farah became the captain of the Black Ferns in 1997. She was the captain of the Black Ferns teams that won the World Cup in 1998, 2002, and 2006. Farah was known as a great leader as well as a great rugby player.

Farah is also a star in the classroom. She's now a director and teacher at Massey University in New Zealand. As a teacher and a student, one of Farah's areas of interest is women's **involvement** in sports.

Overtime!

Farah Palmer only lost one game as captain of the Black Ferns.

Farah Palmer wants to **inspire** young women to be leaders on and off the rugby pitch.

MORE OPPORTUNITIES

If you want to be like Farah or any of the women on the USA Women's Eagles, it's not too early to start playing rugby! Many communities have rugby teams for boys and girls. Try on Rugby is an **initiative** started by USA Rugby to introduce girls and women across the United States to rugby. It **encourages** schools to start girls' rugby teams.

Rugby is a growing college sport in the United States. Rugby clubs also exist for women who want to keep playing the sport as they grow up. In addition, Try on Rugby provides opportunities for women to be rugby coaches and **referees**.

Overtime!

Because rugby is such a tough sport, rugby players must always wear mouth guards. Players can also wear special rugby headgear to **protect** their head.

More girls are playing rugby than ever before! As rugby continues to grow in popularity, there will be even more opportunities for girls and women to find success on the rugby pitch.

PLAY LIKE A GIRL!

Rugby players are strong and brave. They're not afraid to get in a scrum or hold on tight during a ruck. Today, women's rugby players are showing the world that men aren't the only ones who are strong and brave enough to play such a rough sport. They believe the best way to play rugby is to play like a girl!

If you're interested in trying out this tough sport, ask an adult if there are any rugby teams at your school or in your community. The rugby pitch is a great place to make friends as you work together to win!

GLOSSARY

bounce: To spring back or up after striking a surface.

compete: To try to win something that someone else is also trying to win.

competition: An event between two or more people or groups to find a winner.

contact: The state that exists when two people touch each other.

encourage: To try to win over to a cause or action.

initiative: An act or strategy to improve a situation.

inspire: To move someone to do something great.

involvement: The act of being a part of something.

legend: A story coming down from the past that is popularly accepted but cannot be checked.

protect: To keep safe.

referee: A sports official who often has final authority in how a game is conducted.

similar: Almost the same as something else.

INDEX

B
backs, 10

C
conversion, 12, 15

D
drop goal, 12, 14

F
football (American),
    8, 13
football (soccer), 4, 6
forwards, 10

K
knock-on, 10, 15

L
line-out, 8, 9, 15

M
Massey University,
    18
maul, 15

N
New Zealand, 14, 16,
    17, 18
New Zealand Black
    Ferns, 16,
    17, 18

O
Olympics, 4, 16, 17

P
Palmer, Farah, 18,
    19, 20
penalty goal, 12, 14
penalty kick, 12

R
ruck, 15, 22
rugby league, 14, 15,
    16
Rugby School, 6
rugby sevens, 14, 15,
    16
rugby union, 14,
    15, 16

S
scrum, 10, 11, 15, 22

T
touch lines, 8, 9
try, 12, 13, 14, 15

U
USA Women's
    Eagles, 6, 16,
    17, 20

W
Webb Ellis, William, 6
World Cup, 16, 18

WEBSITES

Due to the changing nature of Internet links, PowerKids Press has developed
an online list of websites related to the subject of this book. This site is
updated regularly. Please use this link to access the list:
www.powerkidslinks.com/gjt/rugby